Published by IYYUN Publishing
232 Bergen Street
Brooklyn, NY 11217

http:/www.IYYUN.com

Iyyun Publishing books may be purchased for educational, business or sales promotional use. For information please contact: contact@IYYUN.com

menorah image: Michoel Muchnik
cover and book design: Rochie Pinson

pb ISBN 978-0-6155639-0-9

Pinson, DovBer 1971-
Eight Lights: 8 Meditations for Chanukah / DovBer Pinson

1. Judaism 2. Spirituality 3. Self-help

This book is dedicated
in honor & loving memory of

CHANA ELKON ז"ל

A woman filled with light and love.

EIGHT LIGHTS

CONTENTS

EIGHT LIGHTS

Introduction

Chanukah — with its unique combination of history, ritual, food and fun — is truly one of the most accessible holidays on the Jewish Calendar. But it is also one of the deepest and most meaningful.

From the revolutionary historical events of the Chashmon-ayim, to the social and psychological dangers of assimilation, to the existential aspects of faith, courage and independence — the story of Chanukah is at once exciting and eternally relevant as it describes both the salvaging and security of the Jewish people in a time of national distress.

Many books have been written about Chanukah attempting to tease out all of the various elements that make up this mysterious and miraculous holiday.

So why another book about Chanukah? What still needs to be said?

The mission of this particular book is two-fold: 1) To present the inner aspects of both the seasonal and spiritual dimensions of Chanukah. 2) To provide the active seeker of experiential truth with a series of meditations designed to deepen their understanding of the 'light' of Chanukah.

An honest attempt has been made, in the first two chapters of this book, to lay a conceptual foundation based upon the history and symbolism of Chanukah as it is reflected in the natural world.

This is followed by a brief overview of the ritual of lighting the Menorah, accompanied by all the necessary blessings.

INTRODUCTION

The next section of the book introduces a series of eight meditations. Each meditation is introduced by an 'illumination' to help guide one on their journey beyond the words of the text.

These meditations are intended to be utilized as 'portals into the light of Chanukah'. They should be practiced after the blessings and lighting of the Menorah.

The book then finishes with an elaborate exploration of various spiritual, psychological and historical aspects of the dreidel.

It is our sincerest prayer that this new book about our beloved Chanukah helps to shed and spread new light on an ancient tradition.

EIGHT LIGHTS

CHAPTER I

What is Chanukah?

*M*ai *Chanukah*, asks the Talmud. "What is Chanukah?" This question itself can be a powerful meditation.

The Talmud then informs us:

"On the twenty-fifth day of the month of Kislev begins the days of Chanukah, which are eight, on which lamentation for the dead and fasting are prohibited. For when the Greeks (Assyrians) entered the Temple, they defiled all the oils therein, and when the Chashmonayim (the Hasmonean dynasty) prevailed against

them and defeated them, they searched and found only one cruse of oil which had the seal of the High Priest, which contained oil sufficient for one day's lighting only; yet a miracle occurred and they lit the Menorah (the Temple candelabrum) for eight days. The following year, these days were appointed as a holiday to sing praise, and offer thanks."[Shabbas, 21b]

Chanukah is one of the best known and perhaps most celebrated holidays of the year. It is a festive, family-oriented holiday that comes in an appropriate season: when the days have become the shortest and the desire to connect with family and friends is greatest.

GOING DEEPER

But isn't there more to Chanukah than this? The Talmud's straight-forward response to such an open ended question leaves one wondering if there isn't more going on beneath the surface of such a basic run-down of the 'facts'. And one does not need to enter into a deep state of meditation in order to realize that Chanukah is well known, widely popular and occurs during the winter.

What happens if one takes the time to look deeper into the individual components of the Talmud's reply, or actually contemplates the correspondence between our inner consciousness and the external world.

For it is the style of the Talmud to conceal great depth within minimal breadth. And the Hebrew language contains a beautiful remez, or 'hint', that can help us better understand the integral connection between psyche and surroundings.

In biblical Hebrew, the physical 'world' is referred to as Olam. As is often the case in Hebrew, the word Olam has a variety of subtle permutations and meanings. One of the alternative meanings for the word Olam is 'hidden'.

This linguistic hint illuminates a significant spiritual truth.

Namely, that G-d is both hiding from, and hidden within, the world.

This is further revealed by a simple gematria. The Hebrew word for 'nature', HaTeva, equals 86. This is equivalent to one of the many names of God, Elokim.

Elokim expresses the immanent and creative aspect of G-d's Transcendent Unity. In Beresheit, or 'Genesis', it is the Elokim aspect of Hashem that creates the Heavens and the Earth.

Creation both reveals and conceals the Creator.

Throughout the course of the following pages we will continue to journey deeper into the depths of our initial question: Mai Chanukah, 'what is Chanukah?'

SEASONAL CONTEXT

During the summer, people are generally more outgoing and extroverted, and they take themselves more lightly. However, as the sunlight begins to dwindle and the days begin to get colder, people tend to gravitate inward and begin hibernating, as it were. After the month of Tishrei, with its relatively pleasant weather (around September and October) and its joyful holidays and celebrations, the month of Cheshvan comes along with rainy, colder weather, and a void of holidays. During this period, people desire more often to be alone, to introspect and self-generate.

The majority of the subsequent month follows the same pattern. In Kislev, the days continue to get shorter and colder until we reach the winter solstice, the longest night of the year, which is near the end of the month. At that point in the calendar, a tiny glimmer of light begins to appear and daylight slowly begins to replace the darkness of night. At the same time, a desire resurfaces in people to reconnect with others and to celebrate together. Right around this first glimmer of light and increased connectivity, Chanukah begins.

THE DARKEST MOMENT

Not only does the period of Chanukah contain the winter solstice and longest night of the solar year, but according to the lunar calendar it also contains the darkest nights.

For the longest night of the year is not necessarily the darkest. If, for example, the longest night of the year would fall out at the mid-point of the lunar cycle—on the fifteenth of the month—the night might be the longest, but there will still be some moonlight. However, the time of least moonlight is during the last week of each monthly cycle.

Therefore, since Chanukah occurs in the last week of Kislev, the nights of Chanukah have the least sunlight as well as the least moonlight.

Rabbi Yaakov Yosef, a student of the Baal Shem Tov, calculates that the night the Chashmonayim were victorious—the night they found a small jug of oil and lit the Menorah—was precisely the longest night of the year, on that year.

～

THE SPIRAL OF TIME

After the Talmud briefly describes the story of Chanukah, as above, it concludes: *"The following year, these days were appointed as a holiday...."*

In other words, the holiday of Chanukah was only established on the first anniversary of the miracles.

When the cold and dark season came around again next

year, the sages realized that the very same miraculous energies were again available.

Time flows cyclically with the reoccurring seasons of the year, and also linearly, progressively moving forward.

The best way to describe time, therefore, is not as cyclical or linear, but rather as a spiral. It is both cycling and simultaneously progressing forward or evolving upward.

It follows that each year when Chanukah arrives, it actually brings a higher, more evolved version of the original miracle-producing energy.

Indeed, we do not merely celebrate miracles of the past. The Hebrew Bible, as well as the Oral Tradition, is full of miraculous occurrences. But not every miracle warrants a yearly ritual 'observance'. There is no holiday, for instance, that specifically commemorates the miracle of the Manna, or the miraculous Well of Miriam in the Desert.

The holidays we do celebrate that recall a past event, do so in such a way that we are able to re-experience that archetypal energy in the present moment.

We can then experience that energy more and more vividly each year, as the world spirals ever closer toward the ultimate Redemption.

TRUSTING THE LIGHT

The ninth month of the Jewish year is *Kislev*. In the Torah we find that the etymological root of the word Kislev means 'trust' and 'hope'. Most experiences in life call for some measure of trust.

For example, you might arrange an important meeting with someone at a particular time and place. You have to trust, based on past experience, that the person will be there and at the appropriate time. Realistically, in such a situation, you may be 'taking a chance'. However, through trust, you feel completely confident that the meeting will work out.

The Hebrew word for trust is *bitachon*. Bitachon is an absolute conviction and hope, not only that things can work out, but that they will.

The month of Kislev, and the time of year in which it occurs, embodies this idea of bitachon.

At first, in the earlier parts of the month, the daylight is getting shorter. As this happens, a feeling of depression may set in. Lack of sunlight can lead to Seasonal Affective Disorder, or at least a feeling of melancholy. Everything looks bleak. But just when the season has attained its crescendo with the winter solstice, a small but drastic turn occurs and daylight begins to return again.

This glimmer of warm light, appearing at the end of a period of cold darkness, is sufficient enough to relieve a person of his winter depression and give him hope in a brighter future.

The Chanukah story and symbolism of 'kindling lights within darkness' is spiritually rooted within the context of the season in which it occurs.

⌒

THE REAL MIRACLE

The Chashmonayim had incredible bitachon to stand up to the Greek oppressors who vastly outnumbered them. But it was even deeper bitachon to believe in the possibility of a miracle at the darkest moment, when the Temple was in shambles and the Land of Israel in chaos. Apparently, everything holy had been violated and rendered impure. Many people would have interpreted that reality as hopeless.

Given these circumstances, it would have been understandable had they rejected even the thought of looking for pure oil to kindle the Menorah.

The real miracle therefore was their resolute, logic-defying bitachon. Only because they looked for it, did they find the pure oil. Also because of their trust and positive thinking, one night's worth of oil lasted a full eight nights—the entire time that they needed it to last while re-dedicating the Temple.

Through their miraculous bitachon, they were able to light up the deepest darkness.

⌒

ETERNAL LIGHT

When the Chashmonayim lit this oil of miraculous bitachon, it unleashed the most powerful light of the universe, the *Ohr ha-Ganuz*, the primordial 'Hidden Light'.

This light has no need to burn or consume any substance such as oil in order to shine. This is why the lights remained lit long after a single jug could physically allow.

In order for physical fire to exist, it must destroy its fuel. Similarly, all physical organisms must devour other organisms in order to live.

The Ohr ha-Ganuz, however, is entirely independent and self-sufficient. Moshe (Moses) encountered the same primordial light at the Burning Bush. He thought he saw a bush on fire, and yet the bush was not consumed.

The light that the Chashmonayim revealed in the Temple is a light that does not negate anything. Paradoxically, it does not even negate darkness, rather it shines within even the deepest darkness. The circumstances in Jerusalem continued to be difficult and chaotic, and eventually the Temple was destroyed. However, the revelation of indestructible light continued.

Every year when Chanukah comes, we are given the wonderful ability to increase the revelation of this hidden light—the eternal light that shines within both darkness and light.

∽

BALANCING DARKNESS AND LIGHT

Chanukah is a mid-winter holiday that commemorates the rededication of the Holy Temple. Tisha B'Av is a mid-summer commemoration of the destruction of the Temple.

EIGHT LIGHTS

As the physical light is most revealed during the summer, we enter into the darkest point of the year, spiritually speaking. This is represented by the destruction of the Holy Temple on Tisha B'Av.

Conversely, when the seasonal darkness is at it's most tangible during the winter, we begin to 'kindle the light' and 'rededicate the Holy Temple'. This is the work of Chanukah. This calendrical counter-balance demonstrates the profound seasonal and spiritual symmetry that is expressed by the Hebrew calendar.

Tisha B'Av is the point of darkness within the light of summer, and Chanuakah is the point of light within the darkness of winter.

⌒

LIGHT OF INSPIRATION

It is common for people to be inspired by a challenge and rise to the occasion.

There are moments in each person's life when their inner 'oil' of purity is awakened and it shines brightly. Unfortunately, however, these can be mere peak moments or temporary flashes of inspiration. When the high is over, many people plummet back into their small self.

Each day of the week brings a different shade of experience. Some of us experience spiritual inspiration on Shabbat, while Friday is a completely different story. Some feel relaxed and happy on Sundays, but tense and unhappy on Mondays.

Part of the miracle of Chanukah was that the Chashmonayim were able to kindle the Menorah for eight consecutive nights. They kept up their inspiration, hope and faith for eight days—extending beyond the natural cycle of the week. If Chanukah began on Sunday Night, the last night was again Sunday Night, and yet they were still inspired as if it was the first night.

Even the following year, the sages realized that the light and inspiration of Chanukah had not died out. It was clearly timeless. Thus they established Chanukah as a holiday for all generations and for all time.

Unlike all Biblically-based holidays, at the end of Chanukah there is no havdalah or 'separation' service.

The deeper reason for this is that the light and bitachon of Chanukah are available throughout the year. The light of Chanukah is not separate from any condition or experience.

May we be aware of this hidden light permeating all of our lives, and all of creation, throughout the entire year.

Now that we have taken some time to look a bit deeper into the seasonal and spiritual context of Chanukah, let us now turn our attention to the actual content of the holiday's meditation- the lights.

CHAPTER II
Lights of the Menorah

Light speaks to us in a deep way, particularly the gentle lights that dance atop candles. There are few visual images that are as warming as the image of a flame. Candlelight is pure, simple, luminous and ethereal.

Lights and festivities naturally go together. When people want to express joy, they often use light, from fireworks to birthday cake candles, from romantic candle-lit dinners to colorful, flashing party bulbs.

Just before the beginning of Shabbat and Holiday evenings, we mark the auspicious moment with the illumination of holy candles. Shabbat candles are dedicated both for the honor of Shabbat, and for the pleasure of Shabbat—so that we will eat our Shabbat meal in their pleasant glow, rather than stumble in darkness. On Holidays and Festivals, candles inaugurate the great joy of the day.

In contrast, tradition states that the candles of Chanukah are not meant to be used for our personal pleasure or benefit whatsoever.

One may only 'gaze' at them. In the words of the prayer following the lighting ceremony,

> *"These lights are holy; permission is not granted to*
> *utilize them, but only to look at them."*

In fact, in order to avoid benefiting from these lights, another light or candle must be lit in the room, ensuring that the light of the Menorah is not what allows us to see surrounding objects.

What is the inner meaning of these guidelines? Chanukah lights are not a 'means', but are an end unto themselves. That is, the spiritual intensity of these lights does not allow them to serve as a channel for an extrinsic purpose, no matter how lofty that purpose may be.

Maimonides writes that these lights are intended only "to manifest and reveal the miracle". They exist only in order to draw our focus to the realm of the miraculous; they are dedicated tools of meditation.

In deed, the practice of 'candle gazing' is one of the oldest and most commonly found forms of meditation throughout the world's various cultures and spiritual paths. It is a simple and subtle exercise used to sensitize the seeker of truth to the more spiritual dimensions of the physical world.

And since looking at the lights is all that is traditionally allowed, many sages throughout the centuries have suggested that we do spend some time meditatively gazing at them.

INTRODUCTION

Rabbi Alexander Ziskind suggested that a person sit near the Menorah and sing the Creator's praise. Chassidic teachings say that looking at the lights can heal and rectify all negativity accumulated within our sense of sight—therefore we should spend time gazing at the candles, allowing the light to fill our eyes and purify our vision.

Other sages recommend learning Torah while sitting next to the Menorah, and some recommend simply sitting next to the Menorah and relaxing into an introspective state.

Chabad sources say that looking at the Menorah is an ideal opportunity to contemplate the verse *Ein od mi-L'vado*, "There is nothing else besides *Hashem* (God)."[*Devarim, 4:35*]

Another simple way to meditate with the Chanukah lights is to sit next to them, look at them, and listen to their story.

Do not 'utilize' the lights even for contemplating other concepts; focus your whole attention on the story of the light itself.

EIGHT LIGHTS

In the following chapter we will introduce the traditional blessings to be said before lighting the Menorah. We will then explore a series of meditations intended to accompany our kindlings.

CHAPTER III

The Blessings and Prayers of the Menorah and General Instructions for Menorah Lighting

Many people place the Menorah on the windowsill. Others place their Menorah in the doorway opposite the Mezuzah—that is, near the left doorpost.

The Menorah should be lit each night of Chanukah after nightfall, except on Fridays, when we light the Menorah before sunset.

On the first night of Chanukah, light one candle. Light two candles on the second night and three on the third night, etc.

The candles (or oil and wick) are placed in the Menorah from right to left, although they are lit from left to right.

On the first night of Chanukah, place the candle on the far right side of the Menorah. On the second night, place two candles in the two far right branches, and begin by lighting the newest candle, which is the second from the right. On each subsequent night, light the newest candle first and continue lighting them from left to right.

{fig.a} *order of lighting, day 2*

Gather the family, or all people in the household around the Menorah.

A *shamash* or helper-candle is used to light the Menorah. The Chanukah candles themselves should not be used to light each other.

The shamash or another light in the room will help ensure that you are not using the candles for other than their specific purpose.

The candles should burn at least a half hour into the night.

Since they are for the purpose of publicizing the miracles of Chanukah, they should be burning at a time when other people are capable of seeing them—either people on the street or in your home, or both.

EIGHT LIGHTS

Because women played a key role in the salvation of Chanukah, women and girls are particularly encouraged to rest from all work for at least a half hour while the lights are burning.

Before you light the candles, recite the appropriate blessings.

On the first night of Chanukah (or if it happens to be your first time lighting the Menorah this Chanukah), recite all three blessings.

On all other nights, recite only the first two blessings.

After concluding your blessings, lighting and songs, spend some time sitting near the Menorah. On a weeknight, sit with the candles for a half hour, if possible.

The Menorah Lighting Blessings & Prayers

All three blessings are recited on the first night of Chanukah. (or the first time you light the candles on Chanukah.)
On subsequent nights, only the first two blessings are recited.

1) בָּרוּךְ אַתָּה יְיָ, אֱלֹהֵינוּ מֶלֶךְ הָעוֹלָם, אֲשֶׁר
קִדְּשָׁנוּ בְּמִצְוֹתָיו, וְצִוָּנוּ : לְהַדְלִיק
נֵר חֲנֻכָּה .

2) בָּרוּךְ אַתָּה יְיָ, אֱלֹהֵינוּ מֶלֶךְ הָעוֹלָם, שֶׁעָשָׂה
נִסִּים לַאֲבוֹתֵינוּ, בַּיָּמִים הָהֵם בִּזְמַן הַזֶּה.

3) בָּרוּךְ אַתָּה יְיָ, אֱלֹהֵינוּ מֶלֶךְ הָעוֹלָם, שֶׁהֶחֱיָנוּ
וְקִיְּמָנוּ וְהִגִּיעָנוּ לִזְמַן הַזֶּה:

EIGHT LIGHTS

Transliteration:

1) Ba-ruch A-tah Ado-nai E-lo-he-nu Me-lech ha-olam a-sher ki-de-sha-nu be-mitz-vo-sav ve-tzi-va-nu le-had-lik Ner Cha-nu-kah.

2) Ba-ruch A-tah Ado-nai E-lo-he-nu Me-lech ha-olam she-a-sa ni-sim la-avo-sei-nu ba-ya-mim ha-hem bi-zman ha-zeh.

3) Ba-ruch A-tah Ado-nai E-lo-he-nu Me-lech ha-olam she-heche-ya-nu ve-ki-yi-ma-nu ve-higi-a-nu liz-man ha-zeh.

Translation:

1) Blessed are You, Ado-nai our G-d, King of the universe, Who has sanctified us with His commandments, and has commanded us to Kindle the Chanukah light. 2) Blessed are You, Ado-nai our G-d, King of the universe, Who made miracles for our ancestors in those days, at this season.

3) Blessed are You, Ado-nai our G-d, King of the universe, Who has kept us alive, sustained us, and brought us to this season.

After reciting the appropriate blessings and lighting the candles, the following paragraph is recited or sung:

הַנֵּרוֹת הַלָּלוּ אָנוּ מַדְלִיקִין, עַל הַתְּשׁוּעוֹת, וְעַל הַנִּסִּים,
וְעַל הַנִּפְלָאוֹת, שֶׁעָשִׂיתָ לַאֲבוֹתֵינוּ בַּיָּמִים הָהֵם
בַּזְּמַן הַזֶּה, עַל יְדֵי כֹּהֲנֶיךָ הַקְּדוֹשִׁים. וְכָל שְׁמוֹנַת יְמֵי
חֲנֻכָּה, הַנֵּרוֹת הַלָּלוּ קֹדֶשׁ הֵם, וְאֵין לָנוּ רְשׁוּת
לְהִשְׁתַּמֵּשׁ בָּהֶן, אֶלָּא לִרְאוֹתָן בִּלְבָד, כְּדֵי לְהוֹדוֹת
וּלְהַלֵּל לְשִׁמְךָ הַגָּדוֹל, עַל נִסֶּיךָ וְעַל נִפְלְאוֹתֶיךָ וְעַל
יְשׁוּעוֹתֶיךָ:

Transliteration:

Ha-nei-ros ha-la-lu a-nu mad-li-kin,

Al ha-te-shu-os ve-al ha-ni-sim ve-al ha-nif-la-os,

She-a-si-sa la-avoi-sei-nu ba-ya-mim ha-heim biz-man ha-zeh,

Al ye-dei ko-ha-ne-cha ha-ke-do-shim.

Ve-chol she-mo-nas ye-mei cha-nu-kah ha-nei-ros ha-la-lu ko-desh hem,

Ve-ein la-nu re-shus le-hish-ta-meish ba-hen,

E-la lir-o-san bil-vad, ke-dei le-ho-dos u-le-ha-leil le-shim-cha ha-ga-dol, al ni-se-cha ve-al nif-le-o-se-cha ve-al ye-shu-o-se-cha.

Translation:

We kindle these lights (to commemorate) the saving acts, miracles and wonders which You have performed for our ancestors, in those days at this season, through Your holy priests. Throughout the eight days of Chanukah, these lights are sacred, and we are not permitted to make use of them, but only to look at them, in order to express thanks and praise to Your great Name, for Your miracles, for Your wonders, and for Your salvations.

Many have the custom to also sing Maoz Tzur. Here is the first stanza, with transliteration and translation. This song may be found in most prayer books.

מָעוֹז צוּר יְשׁוּעָתִי לְךָ נָאֶה לְשַׁבֵּחַ
תִּכּוֹן בֵּית תְּפִלָּתִי וְשָׁם תּוֹדָה נְזַבֵּחַ
לְעֵת תָּכִין מַטְבֵּחַ מִצָּר הַמְנַבֵּחַ
אָז אֶגְמֹר בְּשִׁיר מִזְמוֹר חֲנֻכַּת הַמִּזְבֵּחַ.

Transliteration:

Ma-oz tzur y'shu-a-si le-cha na-eh l'sha-bei-ach.
Ti-kon beis t'fi-la-si v'sham to-da n'za-bei-ach.
L'eis ta-chin mat-bei-ach mi-tzar ham-na-bei-ach,
Az eg-mor b'shir miz-mor cha-nu-kas ha-miz-bei-ach.

Translation:

O mighty stronghold of my salvation, to praise You is a delight.
Restore my House of Prayer and there we will bring a thanksgiving offering.
When You will have prepared the slaughter for the blaspheming foe,
Then I shall complete with a song of hymn, the dedication of the Altar.

The concluding stanzas in the Hebrew.

רָעוֹת שָׂבְעָה נַפְשִׁי

חַיַּי מֵרְרוּ בְקֹשִׁי

וּבְיָדוֹ הַגְּדוֹלָה

חֵיל פַּרְעֹה   וְכָל זַרְעוֹ

בְּיָגוֹן כֹּחִי כִּלָּה

בְּשִׁעְבּוּד מַלְכוּת עֶגְלָה

הוֹצִיא אֶת הַסְּגֻלָּה

יָרְדוּ כְאֶבֶן מְצוּלָה.

דְּבִיר קָדְשׁוֹ הֱבִיאַנִי

וּבָא נוֹגֵשׂ וְהִגְלַנִי

וְיֵין רַעַל מָסַכְתִּי

קֵץ בָּבֶל   זְרֻבָּבֶל

וְגַם שָׁם לֹא שָׁקַטְתִּי

כִּי זָרִים עָבַדְתִּי

כִּמְעַט שֶׁעָבַרְתִּי

לְקֵץ שִׁבְעִים נוֹשַׁעְתִּי.

כְּרֹת קוֹמַת בְּרוֹשׁ בִּקֵּשׁ

וְנִהְיְתָה לוֹ לְפַח וּלְמוֹקֵשׁ

רֹאשׁ יְמִינִי נִשֵּׂאתָ

רֹב בָּנָיו   וְקִנְיָנָיו

אֲגָגִי בֶּן הַמְּדָתָא

וְגַאֲוָתוֹ נִשְׁבָּתָה

וְאוֹיֵב שְׁמוֹ מָחִיתָ

עַל הָעֵץ תָּלִיתָ.

יְוָנִים נִקְבְּצוּ עָלַי

וּפָרְצוּ חוֹמוֹת מִגְדָּלַי

וּמִנּוֹתַר קַנְקַנִּים

בְּנֵי בִינָה   יְמֵי שְׁמוֹנָה

אֱזַי בִּימֵי חַשְׁמַנִּים

וְטִמְּאוּ כָּל הַשְּׁמָנִים

נַעֲשָׂה נֵס לַשּׁוֹשַׁנִּים

קָבְעוּ שִׁיר וּרְנָנִים.

חֲשֹׂף זְרוֹעַ קָדְשֶׁךָ

נְקֹם נִקְמַת עֲבָדֶיךָ

כִּי אָרְכָה לָנוּ הַשָּׁעָה

דְּחֵה אַדְמוֹן   בְּצֵל צַלְמוֹן

וְקָרֵב קֵץ הַיְשׁוּעָה

מֵאֻמָּה הָרְשָׁעָה

וְאֵין קֵץ לִימֵי הָרָעָה

הָקֵם לָנוּ רוֹעִים שִׁבְעָה.

CHAPTER IV
Eight Meditations

Jewish meditation spans many methodologies, from the most complex mystical and scriptural contemplations, to the most simple and direct forms of self-inquiry. They are each informed and enriched by deep Torah wisdom.

In the sections that follow we will explore eight meditations on the lights of the Menorah, through both Torah wisdom and practical instruction. It is recommended that one use a different meditation on each night of Chanukah—first study it, and then perform it after lighting your Menorah.

EIGHT LIGHTS

Meditation 1
MIRACLES

After lighting the Menorah we recite a prayer:

"Throughout the eight days of Chanukah, these lights
are sacred, and we are not permitted to 'make use' of them,
but only to look at them, in order to express thanks
and praise to Your great Name for Your miracles,
Your wonders and Your salvations."

When we light the Menorah we express thanks and praise to the Creator for the miracles of the past, as well as for all the miracles unfolding in our present lives right now.

Therefore, when we sit by the Menorah after lighting the candles we should contemplate the historical miracles of Chanukah.

Think about how the *Chashmonayim*, the 'Hasmoneans', had the courage, despite all the chaos of those times, to search for any hidden jugs of pure oil.

Imagine them joyfully finding a jug of pure olive oil with the unbroken seal of the High Priest. Imagine their satisfaction in lighting the Menorah, even if the oil would last only one day.

Now envision their amazement as they realize that the small amount of oil has not gone out, but is miraculously continuing to burn brightly.

Feel their overwhelming awe and gratitude. Sense that through your own lighting tonight, you are drawing down into your life those very same miraculous lights.

Now take a few moments and meditate on all the personal miracles and blessings you have experienced.

Perhaps you have a wonderful spouse, supportive parents and friends, beautiful healthy children, and a healthy body; perhaps you have food to eat, a roof over your head, and air to breathe.

Think about all the love you have ever received. Think of all the gifts that life can offer.

Conclude the meditation by offering thanks and praise to the Master of the Universe for all this kindness.

Miracle Meditation

Find a seat near the lights of the Menorah,
and tune your gaze into their flames.

Begin to bring to mind all of the incredible miracles
which have occurred to us as a people
throughout our collective history.

Draw up some of the miracles which have
occurred in your own life,

Times when you felt the Divine hand guiding you,
times when you were saved from danger,
times when you were full of life and love.
Sit with these miracles and these flames.

Open to the wonder of your life's events,
those big & those seemingly small.

Wonder becomes gratitude; open to wonder.

Meditation 2

HEALING VISION

The lights of the Menorah have the power to heal our eyes, and to rectify and undo the damage of any negative sight or vision.

Find a seat near the lights of the Menorah, and
tune your gaze into their flames.

The flickering fire reflects in your eyes.

If you allow them, they will travel beyond, leaving
their imprint on your inner vision.

As the lights travel inward, let them immerse your
body and mind.

Their pure heat and brilliance cleanses.

The healing light permeates every corner of your
consciousness, clearing away all negative imagery.

The positive image of the candle's quiet fire is with
you in your mind's eye wherever you go.

Meditation 3

ALL IS THE DIVINE LIGHT

Ein od mi-L'vado,
"There is nothing else besides Hashem."
[Devarim 4:35]

'Light' is a metaphor for the Infinite One, the Creator.

Of course, the Creator cannot be contextualized or quantified, nor can conventional language or poetic imagery do justice to That which transcends all definitions.

Yet, aware as we are that it is merely metaphorical, we often refer to Divinity as Ohr Ein Sof, the 'Endless Light'.

'Light' means pure energy or emanation.

On the deepest level there is only the Creator's Light, while from a limited perspective, all matter, time and space are concealing and creating a contrast to this all-pervasive Light.

The universe is not simply a figment of the human imagination, nor is it an illusion. It is an emanation of Divine Light.

The only such illusion is that the world is an independent existence separate from the Source of Light. Just as the Creator manifests Infinity, the Creator also manifests finitude. Both of these rays shine within the Only One.

When we look at the Menorah lights, it is an ideal time to meditate on the Torah's teaching that

Ein od mi-L'vado, "There is nothing else besides Hashem."
[Devarim 4:35]

When we allow the light of the Menorah to fill the entire screen of our vision and imagination, it helps us realize that Divine Light fills and permeates all of Creation.

Just as there appear to be multiple lights on the Menorah, there appear to be separate entities throughout our world.

However, just as we light all the candles from a single flame, all phenomena in the world are sparks of a single fire, expressions of a single Source.

In essence all things are one with the Creator. This includes our very selves, as hinted in Proverbs,

"The candle of Hashem is the human soul."
[Mishlei, 20:27]

All is Light.

'All is Light'
Meditation

Find a seat near the lights of the Menorah, and tune
your gaze into their flames.

As you are filled with the lights of the Menorah,
so is the entire world filled with the Light of the Creator.

There is no real separation.

Is it possible that I myself could be separate from
the One Light, the All?

"The candle of Hashem is the human soul."

Your soul is a flame of the One Fire, the One Source;
in the deepest recesses of your self, you are always
connected as one with the All-Pervasive Light.

Ein od mi-L'vado:
There is nothing but One.

EIGHT LIGHTS

Meditation 4
BEING PRESENT

When we gaze at the lights we may notice that they are
whispering to us, telling us something.
What are they telling us?

One message they are communicating is simply to 'quiet down.' Often, we become so entangled in the noise and rush of day-to-day life, that we fail to notice what is truly important.

We may habitually go about our lives wrapped in stress about the future or anxious regret about the past. This can cause us to neglect focusing on the present moment.

The mind tends to move in all directions.

This is especially true of our generation, since our environment is burgeoning with continuous distractions, such as ringing cell phones, emails, and instant text messages. With all these gadgets and other means of instant gratification, our focus can be so dispersed that we miss being settled in the present moment here and now.

Yet, it is only by being fully in the 'now' that we can change. If we are preoccupied with our past, we are enslaved to a fixed, limited self-image.

If we are preoccupied with our future, we are enslaved to a fixed, limited imagination.

In both cases we are 'stealing' from the present reality.

The gift of life can only be accessed in the 'now', for this is the only moment in which we actually live.

The gentle hissing sound of the Chanukah flames begs us to slow down, relax into the present, and become more introspective.

Listen to the flames, receive their message, and become present with what is.

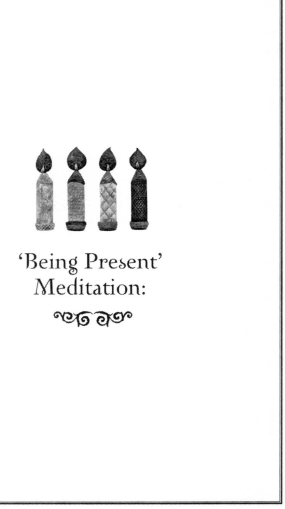

'Being Present'
Meditation:

Find a seat near the lights of the Menorah, and
tune your gaze into their flames.

Relax into the subtle sway of the flames.

The dance of the lights calms the mind.

If the the waves were to cease their ebb and flow
and the sand settled back down to the ocean floor,

how would the presence of stillness feel?

Be present with what is.

Listen to the lights.

EIGHT LIGHTS

Meditation 5
ONENESS OF BODY AND SOUL

Looking at the form of the candle, what do you see?

There are three basic elements:

the flame, the wick, and the oil or wax.

The holy Zohar teaches, "The wick is similar to the body, the flame is analogous to the Divine Presence that rests above the head, and the oil is that which fuses the two together. The oil allows the flame to join and remain connected with the wick—(the oil therefore represents) our good and illuminating deeds." *[Zohar, 3:187a]*

In other words, the flame that reaches upward is our soul, which always yearns for a higher reality. The wick is the physical body, which gravitates earthward. The oil or wax is our good deeds, which allow for a full integration between soul and body.

To live a balanced life we need to harmonize and synthesize soul and body. Just as we instinctively tend to the needs of the body, we must tend to the needs of our soul. Just as we seek spiritual wholeness, we must create physical wholeness, for the two are totally interconnected and united.

A Chasidic teaching underlines this truth: *"A small hole in the body can cause a large hole in the soul."*

The Hebrew word nefesh, 'soul' or spirit, is comprised of three letters: nun, pei, and shin. These letters are an acronym for ner, pesilah, shemen—'flame', 'wick', and 'oil'.

Just as a flame cannot manifest without wick and oil, in order to manifest our soul we must attach it to physicality by means of selfless, noble actions.

Our actions are the clearest indicators of whether we are truly living what we believe.

'Oneness of Body and Soul'
Meditation:

The higher, white fire represents the soul and spirituality, which does not need to overwhelm or negate an 'other' in order to exist.

Deeper levels of soul are represented by more transparent shades of white. Near the peak of the flame it becomes so transparent that it is almost invisible, merging into the infinity of space. This is the unchanging, uninfluenced essence of the self that observes or registers the changing self 'below'.

The lower or outermost surface of the self could be called our 'storyline'. This part of us is in a constant state of change and movement. Every moment of our lives, and with every breath, we are constantly moving, shifting back and forth, expanding and contracting.

Metaphysically speaking, we are continually being re-created, becoming embodied, expiring and then re-embodying.

This is the 'lower light' that continuously moves and changes colors.

Within the flickering and leaping of the lower light is a deep impulse to reach upward. This impulse is called *ratzu*, or 'running', corresponding to the yearning within us to expire in ecstasy or ascend from the world to a higher reality, like a moth to a flame.

The steady higher light, which *'rests on the dark light as on a pedestal'*, demonstrates a quiet connectivity with the world below. This represents *shuv*, or 'returning', an awareness that the purpose of life is in this world, here and now.

In the lower, less evolved levels of our psyche, 'running' is expressed as a desire to transcend the world while neglecting the body. Yet in the higher levels of our psyche, our 'running' energy is in total harmony with its divine purpose, which is to be within the world while inspiring transformation.

There is a dynamic tension between 'running' and 'returning', but they are meant to serve and enhance each other.

'Running' ensures an energetic lightness of being that prevents our involvement with world and body from devolving into self-centered pre-occupation or existential anxiety.

'**Returning**' ensures that we are grounded, that we do not neglect the body or slip fully into ecstasy and expire from the world.

On a deeper level, the dark flickering light leaps up and down and therefore can be seen to have both 'running and returning' within it.

The motionless white light can be seen to be beyond 'running and returning' entirely. It doesn't even need to consume an 'other' in order to exist.

Therefore, the white light can be seen to represent the greater context of life, the stillness and unity that is beyond the fluctuating 'storyline' of the world.

The breath is a physiological experience of 'running and returning'. Each exhale represents the desire to 'run', emptying ourselves and expiring, and each inhale is the desire to 'return' to the body and fill ourselves with new energy.

Between every inhale and exhale, as well as between every exhale and inhale, there is a moment of retention when we are neither inhaling nor exhaling.

This motionless state of retention is beyond the 'running and returning' paradigm, yet in a sense it contains both energies. This is the ethereal presence of the 'white fire' within our physiology. Both physical and spiritual wholeness and health depend on a balance of 'running and returning'. This balance may be illustrated in the way we perform the commandment *V'ahavta es Hashem*, "You shall love Hashem...."[*Devarim, 6:8*]

True love includes both drawing close and moving away, both rising upward and returning to the world.

TThis is also demonstrated within the Hebrew letters that spell the word v'ahavta: vav (6), alef (1), hei (5), beis (2), tav

(400), all together have a numeric value of 414.

This sum is twice the value of the word ohr, 'light', since alef (1), vav (6), reish (200), together equal 207.

Genuine love includes two forms of light. One is the fluctuating light of desire and withdrawal, or running and returning. The other is the settled, motionless light of being open to effortlessly receive or self-reveal.

In addition to the dark light and the white light, there is another element to the candle's flame. Just below the dark light, there appears a tiny empty region, a gap between flame and wick.

Ultimately, if we wish to exude light, warmth and wisdom, we must first disappear like this fertile void. When we attain a measure of self-nullification, that is, a transparency of ego, the light which we project outwardly will be a warming, inspiring and gentle brilliance.

'Yearning and Returning' Meditation:

~୨୧ ୬~

Questions to penetrate the core:

Take a few minutes to sit near the lights of the
Menorah. Meditate on the lights and ask yourself
these pointed questions.

What is my deepest *ratzu*, or desire?
What are my aspirations?

Is my desire merely for fame, money, power or physical comfort and pleasure? Or do I yearn for spiritual connection and growth, for something greater?

Do I have a clear sense of *shuv*, returning,
an acute awareness of my purpose in this world?

Do I know what I should be doing in order to live
out my full potential and purpose?

Ask the questions and beckon the answers to come
to the surface, for the answers are within you.
Sit with the honest answers
to these penetrating questions.
With acceptance of your life's current reality,
be open to receive something greater.

Meditation 7
WHERE IS YOUR LIGHT?

The Book of Proverbs says,
"The candle of Hashem is the human soul."
[Mishlei, 20:27]

The soul is our 'higher self'. It is our deepest potential, the part of us that stands above selfishness, aggression and resentment. The soul is the background of our being. It is the light that can guide and focus our life, all our thoughts, emotions, and actions.

The soul is not something we posses, rather it is who we are; it does not belong to us, it *is* us.

Yet, we have the ability to eclipse our light and use its power and energy to wreck havoc and destroy ourselves and others.

While light can bring warmth and comfort like the glow of a fireplace, it can also be a source of destruction and devastation, like the light of a scorching sun. We must choose to harness our internal light to bring love and joy.

The cumulative sum of the lights we kindle throughout the nights of Chanukah is thirty-six (1 + 2 + 3 + 4 + 5 + 6 + 7 + 8 = 36).

EIGHT LIGHTS

The number 36 alludes to the 36 hours that Adam and *Chavah* (Eve) lived in *Gan Eden* (Garden of Eden)—namely, the six hours from their creation on mid-day Friday to the onset of Shabbat, plus the twenty-four hours of Shabbat itself.

During this time, Adam and Chavah were bathed in a higher light, the light of Paradise.

When night fell at the end of Shabbas, they experienced darkness in their lives for the first time. Yearning to return to the higher light of Gan Eden, they kindled a fire, a lower light.

Like Adam and Chavah, our primordial state is to be bathed in the Ohr ha-Ganuz, the 'Hidden Light' of Gan Eden, the light of Oneness. This is the reality of the 'Tree of Life'. The thirty-six lights that we kindle on Chanukah represent the archetypal experience of this primordial light.

After Adam and Chavah ate from the Tree of Knowledge

and Duality, the Creator asked Adam, *"Ayekah?"* – *"Where are you?"*

It is important to note that Hashem's question was not, "What have you done?", but rather, "Where are you?" For surely Hashem, who is all-knowing, was aware of Adam and Chavah's actions.

The question is, essentially, *'What have you done with your life?'*

The Creator asks each one of us this question throughout our lives. Can we tune in and hear an inner voice compassionately challenging us, 'Where are you? What are your priorities? What do you want out of life? Are you living up to your potential?'

Our lives are the direct response to these questions.

The answer comes into greater forcus on the twenty-fifth night of Kislev, the first night of Chanukah, when we begin kindling the lights of the Menorah.

Appropriately, we find that the twenty-fifth word in the Torah is ohr, 'light'. The word Kislev can be divided in two: kes, 'hidden', and lamed-vav, 'thirty-six'.

Chanukah begins on the twenty-fifth night of Kislev, and the twenty-fifth word in the Torah is *ohr*, 'light'.

On Chanukah we reveal the Thirty-Six Hidden Lights of Creation, the light of our innermost self.

The word *ohr*, light, appears in the Torah thirty-six times. This alludes to the fact that in every generation there are thirty-six hidden tzadikim, elevated souls who sustain, nurture and guard the higher lights of Creation.

The Book of Proverbs teaches, *"The tzadik is the foundation of the world."[Mishlei, 10:25]*

Unassuming and virtually unknown, the thirty-six righteous

people of each generation quietly support and illumine the entire universe.

When we kindle the thirty-six Chanukah lights, we tap into Hidden Light of Gan Eden and activate the hidden point of perfect righteousness within ourselves.

By arousing our inner tzadik, we support the wellbeing of the world around us.

The numeric value of the word *ayekah* is thirty-six. With this in mind, the question "Where are you?" is even more pointed:

> *'Where are your thirty-six lights?'*
> *'What have you done with your light?'*

The flames of the Menorah gently whisper to us to turn our attention inward and behold the luminous potential of our souls. If we meditate in this way, we will rediscover a place of Hidden Light deep within us, a light that has always been there.

Where is your Light?
Meditation:

Take a few minutes to sit near the lights of the Menorah.
As you are basking in the gentle lights, ask yourself:

"Ayekah?"

Where am I in this life's journey?

Is my inner tzadik shining forth?

With every new day, with every new breath do I reveal
more light in my life? . . . in this world?

The journey of excavating one's own inner light
can at times be dark,

but inevitably brightens the entire universe for all.

You have light within to bring forth.

Meditation 8

THE FIVE ASPECTS OF LIGHT: A VISUAL YICHUD MEDITATION

There are two main parts of the candle's flame.
To paraphrase again the words of the Zohar,
in 'The Book of Brilliance':

Havayah, sometimes called 'Hashem' or the Tetragrammaton, connotes the changeless, transcendent attribute of Divinity. It often connotes Chesed or 'kindness', since it transcends the world without destroying or negating it. It is the Infinite 'beingness' that allows all things to just be.

3. THE CHANGING LIGHT/E'H-YEH

The light that constantly changes in appearance from blue, to black, to red, corresponds to the Divine name E'h-yeh. This name means, "I will be," which indicates change or evolution. This is because the way Hashem appears to us is always changing and evolving, according to our own fluctuating perspective and level of spiritual evolution.

4. THE RED LIGHT/ELOKIM

The red light that appears within the blue or black light corresponds to the name Elokim. This name indicates the 'concealment' of Hashem in relation to the world.

The letters of Elokim can be rearaanged to spell the phrase, ilam Yud-Hei, 'the silencing of Yud-Hei (Hashem)'. Elokim also alludes to the attribute of *Din* or severity, such as the power of Divinity to consume worldly forces and negate what is not Divine.

5. THE SUBTLE WHITE LIGHT/ADO-NAI

The subtle white light attached to the wick corresponds with the name Ado-nai. As this light is a reflection of the upper white light, the name Ado-nai is like a receptacle for the transcendent name Havayah. When, in the recitation of formal prayers, we come to the ineffable Tetragrammaton, we recite instead this diminished, more tangible reflection, Ado-nai.

ALLUSIONS OF THE DIVINE NAMES

Everything in the world reflects these five dimensions.* *Let's use a tree as an example:*

1. The '**Nameless Essence**' of a tree is the entirety of the tree itself in both form and process, without regard to its attributes. This is tree as pure being, as 'I'.

2. The **Havayah** of a tree is its ineffable existence and boundless presence in the here and now, it's Isness. It is impossible to comprehensively describe a tree, or anything else for that matter. This is tree as object — "I-It".

3. The **E'h-yeh** of a tree is the fact that it is constantly changing, growing, and fluctuating with the seasons. A tree is always 'tree-ing' or becoming. This is tree as action or potential.

4. The **Elokim** of a tree is that it is revealing, through discernment and definition, only 'tree', and thus discarding or concealing everything else. It exerts its existence by negating all that is non-tree. This is tree as description or definition.

5. The **Ado-nai** of the tree is its name, 'tree'. We indicate a tree with this name, even though what a tree really is transcends our linguistic comprehension. This is tree as subject — "I-Thou".

UNIFICATIONS

A *yichud*, or 'unification', is a contemplative method of drawing the power of transcendent Divinity into the manifest world. This method utilizes tools such as letters and their gematria or 'numerical value'.

Here, we will contemplate the three basic ways that the unchanging transcendent light of the Infinite One can unite with the changeable, manifest, finite reality.

1. The yichud of Havayah and E'h-yeh: when the gematria of Havayah (26) is added to the gematria Ehyeh (21), the sum is 47.

2. The yichud of Havayah and Elokim: when Havayah is added to the name Elokim (86), the sum is 112.

3. The yichud of Havayah and Ado-nai: when Havayah is added to Ado-nai (65), the sum is 91.

The total of these three sums, (47 + 112 + 91), is 250. The word *ner*, 'candle' or 'light', also has a numeric value of 250.

Therefore, before we light a Chanukah ner, we can bring to mind these three yichudim.

By doing so, we hope to invite the transcendent light of Havayah to shine within the world and its many manifestations.

There are twenty-five letters in the names used in the above yichudim:

Havayah has four letters, and it appears three times in
the yichudim, = 12.
E'h-yeh has four letters, = 4
Elokim has five, = 5
and Ado-nai has four, = 4
12 + 4 +5 + 4 = 25.
We now have the number twenty-five.

The number 25 in Hebrew is represented by the letters kuf
and hei, spelling the syllable *kah*.

Thus, the word Chanu-kah can thus mean *chanu*, 'rested
upon', *kah*, 'the 25 letters of these three unifications'.

In other words, the light of these three yichudim are to rest
upon, and settle into, our lives.

They are not just conceptual structures; they can be absorbed
and felt.

Therefore, when we recite the word 'Chanukah' in our blessings over the Chanukah lights, we could intend to internalize and feel the illumination represented by these three unifications.

TURNING THE
MEDITATION INWARD

After you light your Chanukah candles, take some time to quietly gaze at them and take their mystical meanings to heart.

A Visual Yichud Meditation:
Part I

THE WHOLE FLAME

"The flame itself" represents what you are in essence, your total 'you-ness', prior to any of your attributes.

Gaze at the flame, and ask yourself,
"Who am I in essence, prior to any of my attributes?"

Now turn your gaze inward, and enjoy a timeless moment of the irreducible you-ness of you.

THE UPPER WHITE LIGHT

The large, white part of the flame represents your inner 'Havayah', your unchanging, transcendent soul that is attached to Hashem.

Gaze at the white light and ask,
"What is the most stable aspect of my life, that which I

hold onto the most, or that which holds me?"

Turn your gaze inwards, and recognize the awesome fact that you are always held in the infinite light, kindness, and 'beingness' of Hashem.

THE BLUE OR BLACK LIGHT

The blue or black light near the base of the flame represents your inner E'h-yeh, your state of yearning, changing and becoming.

Gaze at this light and ask,
"What are my aspirations and dreams? What do I see myself becoming, and what can I do to begin the process?"

Turn your gaze inward, and recognize your yearning to manifest and embody more of your higher self, your transcendent soul.

THE RED LIGHT
WITHIN THE BLUE OR BLACK LIGHT

The red light that sometimes appears within the blue or black light represents your inner Elokim, the element of concealment or negation in your life.

Gaze at this area of the flame and ask,
"What are the negative or destructive habits and thought patterns that I need to refine, reject or release?"

Turn your gaze inward, and recognize any concealment of your soul's brilliance.

THE SMALL WHITE LIGHT
ATTACHED TO THE WICK

The small, white light attached to the wick represents your inner Ado-nai, the way you express your transcendent soul in the world.

Perhaps the medium of this expression is your profession, your family role, or your social identity.

Gaze at the small white light attached to the wick and ask,
"How do I express my true identity in the world? How can I better reflect my soul in thought, word, and action?"

Turn your gaze inward and recognize that your life and story are vehicles for your soul's purpose.

INNER UNIFICATIONS

To draw the unifications within, notice that the upper white light of the flame does not cancel out the lower three lights, nor vice-versa.
On the contrary, all the colors are united in a continuous spectrum of light.

This represents the fact that Havayah is unified with E'h-yeh, Elokim, and Ado-nai.

Now, turning your gaze inward to recognize the fact that your changeless, transcendent brilliance miraculously co-exists with the ups and downs of your life, your ambitions and identifications.

You are one.

A Visual Yichud Meditation:

Part II

*To amplify the five inward meditations above,
here are five simple and direct questions that you could
ponder, as you meditate on the Chanukah lights:*

Who am I?

What is most precious to me?

What are my aspirations and dreams?

What do I need to release from my life?

Am I expressing my higher self
in the world?

CHAPTER V

Meditations on the Dreidel:

Historical, Allegorical, and Kabbalistic Perspectives

On Chanukah, we have a custom of playing with the dreidel. In Hebrew, a dreidel is called s'vivon, 'spinner'.

The dreidel is a small 'top' with four sides, spun from a handle above, and revolving on a pivot below. On each of the four sides, a Hebrew letter is inscribed: Nun, Gimmel, Hei, Shin.

PLAYING DREIDEL

Here is how the game of dreidel is played today.

Each player puts in some candy, chocolate coins, or some change, into the middle, or the 'pot'.

When you spin the dreidel, if it lands on its side with the letter '**gimmel**' 'ג' facing up, you win the whole pot.
If it lands on '**hei**', 'ה' you get half the pot.

'**Nun**' 'נ' means you get nothing, and '**shin**' 'ש' requires that you put another item into the pot.

In Yiddish the four letters inscribed on the dreidel stand for the following: *gimmel* is for *gantz*, you get 'the whole thing'. *Hei* is for *halb*, 'half' the pot. *Nun* is for *nisht*, 'nothing', and *shin* is for *shtell arein*, 'put in'.

THEN AND NOW

In the Land of Israel, during the Roman Era of religious persecution, the study of Torah and the performance of mitzvos were prohibited.

Teachers would gather their young Torah students and hide

in caves or remote areas. As they would study, one child would be on the lookout, and when he noticed a Roman soldier approaching, he would notify the others. They would take out gambling toys and pretend they were playing games. According to legend, they were playing dreidel. Seeing games in progress, the Roman's would not suspect them of studying Torah, and would go on their way.

This is how our intellectual and spiritual tradition survived.*

*Note: The earliest mention of the dreidel or its significance is found in relatively recent texts; perhaps the toy is as old as the late Eighteenth Century. On the other hand, the game of dreidel could be a variation on Teetotum, a much older German gambling game that used a top with four sides. In any case, nothing is mere coincidence; everything is b'hashgachah, by Divine Providence, and the dreidel has been associated with Chanukah for a deeper reason.

FOUR LETTERS

Chanukah is a celebration of our religious freedom.

The dreidel reminds us of a time when our freedom was in peril and yet we miraculously remained dedicated.

The letters on the driedel thus acquired a Hebrew interpretation: nun for nes, 'a miracle', gimmel for gadol, 'great', hei for hayah, 'happened', and shin for sham, 'there'—"A great miracle happened there (in the Land of Israel)."

Appropriately, dreidels in Israel are engraved with the letter pei for poh, 'here'. This indicates that the Chanukah miracles happened 'here', in Israel, as opposed to 'there', as perceived from the perspective of exile.

The letters on the dreidel also represent the two basic mitzvos that we perform on Chanukah: lighting the Menorah for eight nights, and singing Hallel, the Creator's praise, during the day.

Re-arranged, nun, gimel, hei and shin are an acronym for *Neiros Shemonah*, 'eight lightings', and *Hallel Gamur*, the 'Complete Hallel' service.

Since the dreidel was a means of concealing the Torah-study of children, it is a symbol of spiritual defiance and perseverance in the face of adversity.

The four sides and four letters therefore came to represent the four general empires that attempted to destroy the Jewish People: the Babylonians, Persians, Greeks and Romans.

Later, we will explain the significance of these four empires, and the corresponding exiles in more detail.

Ever since the destruction of the Second Temple, we have been in a spiritual condition of galus, or 'exile'.

Our present state of galus is considered to be an extension

of the Roman Exile.

Much like the spinning dreidel, which eventually falls down, these four empires that once sought to enslave and conquer us eventually fell themselves.

Defying all odds, we remained standing.

A METAPHOR FOR LIFE

The means of our survival has always been a relentless cleaving to our center, and to the Divine Center-point of all reality.

When the dreidel is spinning intensely around its center, the four sides blur and appear circular; the multiple surfaces of the cube become as the single surface of a cylinder, as they cleave, so-to-speak, to the oneness of their center.

Like the dreidel, we only topple when we loosen our intrinsic bond with our Center-point, and aspire to act independently of our Source.

When we cling to the square outer sides of the dreidel, instead of to the Center-point, our life can seem to be spinning out of control.

We may occasionally notice a coherent pattern or internal structure to our unfolding life story, but more often, life seems haphazard or random. One day we are oriented to the right, the next day to the left; one moment we seem to be in full control of our lives, and the next moment we seem to be controlled by outside forces. It seems like a gamble, whether we will be winners or losers.

This is the experience of personal exile.

Yet, as the dreidel gently shows us, this is how our lives might be perceived from 'below'. There is also a hand 'above' that sets the dreidel of our lives into motion.

Therefore, even when events appear to be whirling out of focus, we can strive to realize that nothing is in essence random or chaotic. Everything is guided from above by the Divine will.

Often salvation arises *k'heref ayin*, 'as swift as the blink of an eye'.

One moment, the prospects of our future can seem utterly hopeless. Then, as if from nowhere a ray of light can appear, radically changing our orientation.

When we are aware that we could be illumined at any moment, we realize that the Creator is spinning the dreidel of life.

Within the story of Chanukah, we can easily see the higher miracles and the supernal hand.

When we purify our hearts and consciousness, we can also observe our own lives as from 'above'.

⌒

THE NATURE OF NATURE

The whole universe pulses with the rhythm of life and death, and all things are in a constant stage of flux, putting on and shedding forms, for nothing within the sphere of created existence is everlasting or permanent.

Even at a sub-nuclear level, the quarks and gluons that make up the atoms of our bodies are perpetually annihilated and re-created. Ninety-eight percent of the atoms in your body were not there one year ago. Your skin is renewed every month, your stomach lining every four days, and the surface cells that actually contact food are new every five minutes.

All of existence is like a whirling dreidel.

The Jewish sages called the universe a *galgal ha-chozer*, a rotating wheel. What is up one day is down the next, and vice versa.

Yet while everything is in a constant state of becoming, of turning and shifting, many people stubbornly cling to rigid, linear definitions of life.

This attempt to fix reality upon unmoving or predicable reference points is related to Hellenism, idolatry, and materialism.

It naturally creates much stress and suffering.

SOMETHING AND NOTHING

A rigid approach to life is a symptom of '*yesh*-consciousness'. *Yesh* means 'something'—ego, or the superficial observable layer of finite reality.

The antidote to yesh-consciousness is to include '*ayin*-consciousness' in our lives. Ayin means 'nothing'—egolessness, and oneness with the infinite Divine reality from where the yesh continually springs into existence.

Since our senses are so captivated by 'things', we come to believe that yesh is the only reality.

We lose touch with ayin, otherwise known as the *yuli*, or pure potentiality.

When we are in touch with this infinitely creative reality, the self and the world we perceive never assume rigid or absolute definitions.

Instead, we live in the flow of continuous creation and re-creation.

When we get stuck in a yesh paradigm, we buy into the absoluteness of our condition.

If a person is in a place of darkness—whether spiritually, mentally or even financially—and there seems to be no way out, let him look beyond the yesh into the ayin. The deeper we penetrate beyond the yesh, the more opportunities open to us.

In ayin-consciousness, the laws of cause and effect are suspended, and everything is possible.

The first verse of Psalm 121 is a meditation on this teaching:

Esa einai el he-harim,

I lift up my eyes to the mountains,

me'ayin yavo ezri?

from where (or 'from the ayin') will my help come…

When you lift your eyes to the 'mountains', and you see only the yesh in front of you, you might feel despair.

When all you perceive are mountainous barriers and obstacles, from your depths comes the cry, "From where will my help come?"

Yet, if you look beyond that yesh, you can realize that me'ayin—from the Divine ayin—comes your salvation.

FOUR LEVELS OF SELF

A human being is comprised of four basic elements, or dimensions of yesh, and each one reflects a letter on the dreidel.

GIMMEL is for guf, the 'body', which on its own is inanimate matter.

NUN is for nefesh, 'spirit', the life-force that allows the body to grow and to feel.

SHIN is for seichel, 'mind' or consciousness.

HEI is for ha-kol, the 'all'—the comprehensive soul or transcendent aspect of a person that includes and unifies the three previous elements.

Any of these elements can be thrust into a state of exile when misaligned with the Source.

⌒

FOUR EXILES

The four kinds of misalignment, or four trajectories moving away from center, are embodied by the four empires that sought to destroy our 'centeredness' and to exile the Jewish People.

One empire wished to destroy the bodies of the Jews, one desired to expunge their ability to feel, another sought to corrupt their minds, and another to quench any aspiration or yearning for transcendence.

The conquering Babylonian army destroyed the First Holy Temple and drove most of the Jews out of Jerusalem. They desired to eradicate and extinguish the 'nun', the nefesh of the people. This exile was a devastating trauma to the Jewish People, and to the city that was the center of their life-force.

Once the Jews were exiled to Babylon, the Persian Empire rose to power. It was during this reign that Haman was inspired to rise up and destroy the 'gimmel', the guf of the Jew.

The intellectual and philosophically inclined Greeks attacked the 'shin', the seichel of the Jew, by instituting Hellenic thought and forbidding Torah-study.

The 'pei' of the Israeli dreidel stands for philosofiya, 'philosophy'. The Greeks were not out to kill the Jewish body or spirit, but rather to enfold them within the Greek Empire by indoctrinating them and toppling their worldview.

The Roman Empire, with her offspring, Western civilization, has imposed all three expressions of exile upon the world.

Ever since the destruction of the Second Holy Temple, Jews have suffered bodily, spiritually and intellectually—this is the 'hei', or ha-kol of the Jew.

Between the massacres and pogroms, and the threat of assimilation and the enticement of secularism, there has been a constant battle on all fronts between 'Rome' and 'Jerusalem'.

The survival of the Jewish life-force, intellect and soulfulness, is indeed a miracle that we witness with our own eyes.

PERSONAL EXILE

Exile on a personal level might not mean physical or social threat, but it is always linked with a state of mind that limits the full revelation and flow of who we really are.

Just as the dreidel is carved with four surfaces that define its shape, we too have carved ourselves down to a limiting set of self-definitions.

Whether we believe ourselves to be primarily physical, sensate, intellectual, or even transcendent, we have boxed ourselves into an identity, and this creates the appearance of separation from the whole.

This four-sided dreidel of limited identity, however, will one day slow down and topple. The prison of limitations is impermanent.

When we go about arguing in support of our limitations, believing, 'I am not strong enough, I did not have the right upbringing, I am not intelligent enough, I am not spiritual enough'—this may create an appearance of walls and barriers. But it is only an appearance.

ONE REDEMPTION

To break out of any personal limitation or communal exile, there is one main path: to become 'centered'.

From the perspective of the center, all limitations are mere projections or superficial shadows. We have the ability to access this powerful perspective at all times, because deep within our center is the light of Oneness.

Most of the surviving remnants of Israel come from the tribe of Yehudah or 'Judah'.

The name 'Judah' is the source of the words 'Jew' and 'Judaism'; today all Israelites are called Jews or Yehudim. The name Yehudah is comprised of five letters, yud-hei-vav-dalet-hei.

Four of these letters spell the name of Hashem, connoting Divine Oneness: Yud-Hei-Vav-Hei. This suggests that a Yehudi is ultimately rooted and centered in Divine Oneness.

Also within the name Yehudah is the letter Dalet, the fourth letter of the Alef-beis, which hints at the four directions of the world, or the four sides of the dreidel.

When we are consciously centered in the light of Oneness, we can radiate it into all four directions of the world.

The light of Oneness dissolves all shadows, and removes the sharp edges of exile that seem to constrain or threaten us.

When we are in touch with the one Hand that 'spins' all of Creation, we can enter any situation of constriction, and yet remain centered and essentially redeemed.

This is why, in the Biblical narrative, the first son that Yaakov sends into the exile of Egypt is Yehudah.

LIGHT OF THE REDEEMER

Let us look more deeply into the above Biblical narrative.

Yosef has become the ruler of Egypt. He perceives that his brothers desire to release their misaligned intentions, and he hears that their father Yaakov is still alive.

Yosef therefore suggests that his brothers bring Yaakov, and the rest of the Israelite community, from the famine-stricken Land of Israel, to settle in Egypt. Yosef offers them settlement in the Egyptian province of Goshen. The patriarch Yaakov prophetically sees that leaving Israel for Egypt will culminate in harsh exile. Therefore before he takes the Israelites to their settlement, he sends his son Yehudah to *Goshen*, in the words of the Torah, he sends him '*Goshenah*', to scout out the land and see if it is an appropriate place to dwell.

According to Midrash, Yehudah goes there in order to set up a place for Torah-study and spiritual contemplation.

Remarkably, the word Goshenah is comprised of the letters on the dreidel. This suggests that Goshen is a place where the four levels of personal exile, and the four future exiles of the Jewish People, are present in seed form. Yehudah goes into these four letters, so-to-speak, to ensure that the exile will have no existential or permanent bearing on the community.

Being a deeply centered individual, Yehudah is able to enter into a place of constrictions and limitations, and yet remain connected to the light of Oneness deep within himself.

He then shines the four letters of the Name of Hashem into

the Dalet—the four directions—dispersing there the shadows of limitation and exile. He thereby transforms Goshen into a source of redemptive, messianic consciousness.

The word Goshenah has a numerical value of 358 (gimmel=3, shin=300, nun=50, and hei=5). The word Mashiach, 'redeemer' has exactly the same numerical value (mem=40, shin=300, yud=10, and ches=8).
The darkness of Goshen is only an absence of light.
Exile is only a *kelipah*, a 'husk' which conceals the light of Oneness within.

In the narrative of the Tree of Good and Evil, the snake personifies kelipah. In Hebrew, 'snake' is *nachash*, which is also 358.

Eventually, the kelipah of the nachash will fall—the snake will shed its skin, revealing Mashiach.

Likewise, the four-sided dreidel of exile will fall, and the darkness of our 'Goshen' and exile will be revealed as the light of 'Mashiach' or redemption.

The transformation of the nachash into the Mashiach is stimulated by our kindling of the Chanukah lights.

The three blessings we recite upon kindling the lights hint at this process. The three blessings are: "…ner Chanukah" (ches), "…sheasa Nisim" (nun), and "…Shehechiyanu" (shin). These three letters spell the word nachash. When we shine the light of Oneness on the nachash, the force of kelipah and exile is banished.

CIRCLE-REVELATIONS

When a square dreidel is spun, it appears as a circle.

A square represents linear, defined, yesh-consciousness, while a circle, which has no beginning or end, corners or defined points, represents ayin-consciousness, and the breaking of our perceived boundaries and limitations.

The square also represents the 'prose', or the defined storyline of our life, and the circle represents the 'poetry' or music, the non-linear and miraculous aspect of life.

Law and order are 'square', while music and poetry are 'circular'.

The Torah embraces a paradox: it is a book of law, and yet it is also called a *shirah*, a 'song' (*Devarim, 31:19*).

In general terms, however, we can view the Written Torah as a 'square' of Divine law and order, and the Oral Torah, which is revealed through human collaboration, as a 'circle' of poetry, inspiration, and devotion.

With this distinction in mind, we can understand many of the customs that have been revealed within the collective prophetic soul of *Knesses Yisrael*, the Assembly of Israel, otherwise known as the Jewish community.

One example is the inspiring Rabbinic holiday of Chanukah.

Chanukah is not found in the Written Torah. It is a holiday that has sprung from the circle-reality of Jewish creativity.

There two other fully Rabbinic holidays in the calendar: Purim and Simchat Torah. The latter is a much later innovation, perhaps from the early Fourteenth Century, CE. On all three days of Chanukah, Purim and Simchat Torah, we turn the squares of our lives into circles.

On Chanukah, we spin the dreidel, on Purim we spin the gragger, and on Simchat Torah we take out the Torah and dance in circles around the square bimah.

Sometimes we need the boundaries of law and order, and other times we need to whirl with the poetry and passion of being alive.

When we are getting married, for example, the poetry of life takes more prominence.

Although we enter a square wedding canopy and thereby

draw boundaries of an orderly structure around our relationship, we focus on creating circles. The circumambulations of the bride and the circular wedding ring given by the groom symbolize the endless passion and poetry of love.

THE BLESSING OF CHANUKAH

Both our collective freedom and our personal freedom are always available; all we need to do is shine the light of awareness upon the darkness that seems to surround us.

When we reveal our light, every moment of life becomes miraculous and freeing.

When each person reveals enough of their 'centeredness' and light, the darkness and misalignment of our collective exile will vanish.

On the Festival of Lights, we can tap into the light and poetry of life.

We take a dreidel in our hand and give it a spin, affirming our redemption from all limitation in the areas of 'nun'/nefesh/spirit, 'gimel'/guf/body, 'shin'/seichel/mind, or 'hei'/hakol/totality.

This Chanukah, may we open ourselves to new possibilities.

May we spin our 'squares' into 'circles', release our rigid thinking, and embrace the infinite potential that the Creator is continuously giving us.

May we cleave to our Divine Center-point, and radiate the Light of Oneness in all directions.

OTHER BOOKS
BY RABBI DOVBER PINSON

Rabbi Pinson's books are available in all fine book stores and on the web.

REINCARNATION AND JUDAISM:
The Journey of the Soul

A fascinating analysis of the concept of reincarnation as it appears in the works of the Kabbalistic masters, as well as how it is discussed by the great thinkers throughout history. Dipping into the fountain of ancient wisdom and modern understanding, the book addresses and answers such basic questions as: What is reincarnation? Why does it occur? and How does it affect us personally?

INNER RHYTHMS:
The Kabbalah of Music.

The study of music as response is explored in this highly engaging book. Music and its effects in every aspect of our lives are looked at in the perspective of mystical Judaism and the Kabbalah. The topics range from Deveikut/Oneness, Yichudim/ Unifications, merging heaven and earth, to the more personal issues, such as Simcha/Happiness, expressing joy, to the means of utilizing music to medicate the sad soul. Ultimately, using music to inspire genuine transformation.

MEDITATION AND JUDAISM:
Exploring the Jewish Meditative Paths.

A comprehensive work on Jewish meditation, encompassing the entire spectrum of Jewish thought--from the early Kabbalists to the modern Chassidic and Mussar masters, the sages of the Talmud to the modern philosophers--this book includes them all.

The book is both a scholarly, in-depth study of meditative practices, and a practical, easy to follow guide for any person interested in meditating the Jewish way. The word meditation calls to mind the traditional, obvious associations that society has accumulated, such as the lotus position, the mantras and the like. Meditation and Judaism attempts to broaden our view of meditation, demonstrating that in addition to the traditional methods of meditation, meditation is prevalent within so many of the common Jewish practices.

The book also explores a variety of fascinating and intriguing topics such as; panoscopic vision, spiritual synesthesia, psychic powers. What is black magic? What is the Koach HaTumah – the impure powers? What is the definition of spirituality?

TOWARD THE INFINITE:
The Way of Kabbalistic Meditation.

'Toward the Infinite; A Kabbalistic Meditation' focuses exclusively on the Kabbalistic – Chassidic approach to meditation. Encompassing the entire meditative experience, it takes the reader on a comprehensive and engaging journey through meditation.

The journey begins with the readying of oneself for the meditation. The preparatory stage is discussed at length, dealing with issues such as the time of day most conducive to the meditation, the meditative positions and the like. The journey continues with the actual meditative experience. The various states of consciousness that a person encounters in the course of the meditation, beginning at a level of extreme self-awareness and concluding with a total state of non-awareness.

'Toward the Infinite; A Kabbalistic Meditation' is deliberately written to appeal to a mass audience and thus does not make use of scholarly quotations and references. An easy read which will pique the interest of all those intrigued by spirituality and meditation.

JEWISH WISDOM OF THE AFTERLIFE:
The Myths, the Mysteries & Meanings

What happens to us after we physically die? What is consciousness? And can it survive without a physical brain? What is a soul? Can we remember our past lives? Do near-death-experiences prove the immortality of the soul?

Drawing from the fountain of ancient Jewish wisdom and modern understanding of what consciousness is, this book explores the possibilities of surviving death, the near-death-experience, and a possible glimpse of the peace and unconditional love that awaits, empowering the reader to live their day-to-day life with these great spiritual truths.

In 'Jewish Wisdom on the Afterlife', Rav DovBer Pinson explores the possibility of life after death, presenting a basic understanding of what it means to be mortal and how an understanding of our immortality can serve us in the present and empower us to live more meaningfully today.

UPSHERIN:
Exploring the Laws, Customs & Meanings
of a Boy's First Haircut

What is the meaning of Upsherin, the traditional celebration of a boy's first haircut at the age of three? This in-depth answer to that question explores as well the questions: Why is a boy's hair allowed to grow freely for his first three years? What is the kabbalistic import of hair in all its lengths and varieties? What is the mystical meaning of hair coverings? Rav DovBer Pinson answers these questions with his trademark deep learning and spiritual sensitivity. *Includes a guide to conducting an Upsherin ceremony.*

THIRTY–TWO GATES OF WISDOM:
Awakening through Kabbalah:

Kabbalah holds the secrets to a path of conscious aware-ness. In this compact book, Rav DovBer Pinson presents 32 key concepts of Kabbalah and shows their value in opening the gates of perception.

A short excerpt from the introduction: Simply translated, Kabbalah means "that which is received." Looking deeper, the word Kabbalah can mean to be open and receptive, to challenge one's own internal navigational system in order to see, hear, and be open to… more. We must be receptive to a teaching to fully absorb it. We turn ourselves into ves-sels and invite within that which we wish to understand or grasp. In this way, we become receptacles, dispensaries, and a part of the Kabbalah. We become vessels of this tradition by opening the self to a higher reality, and viewing the spirit within the matter. We raise our consciousness to the point where the Divine within all creation is revealed. As we pursue a deeper awareness, we become less ego-cen-tered and more attuned to the deeper significance of our surroundings.

TEFILIN:

*A Guide & Deeper Exploration of the meaning
and Practice of Tefilin*

This is a booklet that was written as a guide to help people put on Tefilin, discussing the basic laws and how one puts on Tefilin, and offers a deeper explanation of the Mitzvah.

THE PURIM READER:

The Holiday of Purim Explored

With a Persian name, a costuming dress code and a woman as the heroine, Purim is certainly unusual amongst the Jewish holidays. Most people are very familiar with the costumes, Megillah and revelry, but are mystified by their significance. Rav DovBer Pinson offers a glimpse into the unknown world of Purim, uncovering the mysteries and offering a deeper understanding of this unique holiday.

THE IYYUN HAGADAH:

An Introduction to the Haggadah

In this beautifully written introduction to Passover and the Haggadah, Rav DovBer Pinson, guides us through the major themes of Passover and the Seder night. Rav Pinson addresses the important questions, such as; What is the big deal of Chametz? What are we trying to achieve through conducting a Seder? What's with all that stuff on the Seder Plate? And most importantly, how is this all related to freedom? His answers will surprise even those who think they already know the answers to these questions.

ב"ה

To
MY BELOVED TEACHER,
MY REBBE

THE LUBAVITCHER REBBE
of blessed memory

His life was dedicated in the
dissemination of light,
and in the belief that this world
will be perfected
one good deed at a time.

CPSIA information can be obtained at www.ICGtesting.com
Printed in the USA
LVOW10*1022031215

465191LV00004B/16/P

9 780615 563909